T0304568

VICTORIAN
PARLOUR GAMES

**A Modern Host's
Guide to Classic Fun
for Everyone**

By Ned Wolfe

Illustrations by Bene Rohlmann

CHRONICLE BOOKS

SAN FRANCISCO

Library of Congress Cataloging-in-Publication Data is available.

ISBN 978-1-7972-3100-6

Manufactured in China.

Design by Maggie Edelman.

Illustrations by Bene Rohlmann.

10 9 8 7 6 5 4 3 2 1

Chronicle books and gifts are available at special quantity discounts to corporations, professional associations, literacy programs, and other organizations. For details and discount information, please contact our premiums department at corporatesales@chroniclebooks.com or at 1-800-759-0190.

Chronicle Books LLC
680 Second Street
San Francisco, California 94107
www.chroniclebooks.com

FOR MY
NEPHEW CALLUM

CONTENTS

INTRODUCTION

One dreary December morning, in that strange, liminal stretch between Christmas and New Year's, I found myself sketching in a Belgian café near Harvard. Eavesdropping is a writer's professional hazard, and as my mind wandered, I found myself listening to the conversations around me.

"What games do you want to play at your party?" a well-dressed woman asked the preteen girl sitting across from her. I didn't have to strain my ears too hard to hear; their table was next to mine.

"I don't know," the girl replied. "Maybe Musical Chairs?"

Her mother nodded, taking notes on her iPhone. Without raising her eyes from her screen, she started giving suggestions. "How about Blind Man's Bluff?" *Buff*, I corrected internally.

Unaware of my silent correction, the mother continued. "That sounds a bit ableist. How about a game where everyone makes farm-animal noises and we have to guess who made what sound?"

Like the family I overheard, most of us unconsciously reach for parlour games with roots in the Victorian era. These games have stood the test of time for good reason. Everyday magazines of the age included game rules, which helped popularize the games and standardized the ways they were played. Even so, some regional differences still remain in the forms of game variations, such as different words to chant, number of players, or even the same name applied to completely different sets of rules.

These games have also survived because they are fun and easy to play. Most are simple and don't require more than a pencil and paper, deck of cards, or some chairs. And the word games ask only for imagination and verbal dexterity. Best of all, many of the games will have the players in stitches. All you have to do is read about the game of Yes and No in *A Christmas Carol*, when Ebenezer Scrooge is savagely burned by his fun-loving nieces and nephews, to imagine your own friends laughingly roasting you in the same way.

As is the cardinal rule of eavesdropping, the eavesdropper doesn't interfere by joining in the conversation. So when I was listening to the family in that café, I resisted the urge to reach out and recommend more games for their party. Games like Smells; Are You There, Moriarty?; and Pin the Tail on the Donkey. Instead, dear reader, I recommend them to you here. Relive the childhood fun of the familiar games and delight in the discovery of some which are new to you. Wallop your friends and family with pillows. Make them smell something strange. Catch their eye and make funny faces until one of you dissolves into giggles.

As you discover the games in this book, I hope you enjoy the fun facts, literary tidbits, and delightful histories I've compiled. There were many that didn't make it, from tales of dueling magazine editors to asides about the intersection of welfare reform and public art. I hope you come away with a different view of the Victorians, where their stuffiness hid a silliness that emerged whenever they entertained.

Most importantly, I hope you play!

PARTY GAMES

CHAPTER 1

PARTY GAMES

The stage is set. The curtains are drawn; candles are lit. The table is set with a Sunday roast. Guests are due to arrive at any minute. Everything is perfect—but what about the evening's entertainment?

The games that follow are wonderful options for medium to large gatherings of friends and family. They are fit for all ages, are fairly easy to play, and mostly require little to no specific setup. While these are not the most dignified of games, even the usually tight-laced Victorians got silly when playing these classic examples of parlour games.

THROWING THE SMILE

Alternative Name: Smile Toss

Number of Players: 4+

. . . .

This is one of many games with a common objective: Don't smile. While simple to explain, it's deceptively difficult to play.

Throwing the Smile is a great game for groups large and small, as it requires no equipment other than the people present. Play it while camping, to pass time while waiting for food at a restaurant, or at a party. Throwing the Smile can be played by all ages, which makes it a wonderful game for multigenerational get-togethers, like birthdays and holiday dinners.

. . . .

HOW TO PLAY:

1. The players sit in a circle. One player is selected to start.

2. Player One smiles for a moment or two, then makes a show of wiping their hand across their face to "remove" the smile.

3. Player One calls another player's name and pretends to throw the smile at them.

4. Player Two "catches" it with their hand, puts it on for a while, and then wipes it off to throw to another player after calling their name.

5. Anyone who smiles out of turn is out. The players who are out all laugh and make faces in order to make the players who are still in smile or laugh out of turn.

6. The last player remaining wins the game.

VARIATIONS:

Throwing the Smile can also be played as a co-operative game. Players can work together to count how many smiles are thrown without someone breaking, or they can set a goal and try to reach it, or play multiple times to try to break a previous record.

There are a couple of ways to identify who is out. Those who are out may stand while the players still in remain seated; however, this is not always accessible for all players. Other options include moving players' chairs (or bums, or pillows) back a foot to remove them physically from the game. Or you could use hats, cups, etc. to indicate who is out.

THE LAUGHING GAME

Number of Players: 2+

. . . .

The Victorian era is stereotyped as a prudish, straitlaced period where Queen and country were perpetually not amused. With this idea in mind, it's quite funny that Victorians needed a game to permit themselves to laugh! In 1875, a man named George Vasey published a book titled *The Philosophy of Laughter and Smiling*. Despite the seemingly positive title, Vasey was vehemently anti-mirth. His book is a treatise on how those who laugh are empty-headed fools.

Fortunately, not everyone held the same philosophy as Vasey. There existed a vibrant community of humor and humorists in Victorian England, with some able to earn a living crafting jokes professionally as comic magazines like *Punch* and *Fun* flourished. It only makes sense that they loved a game in which the player who laughs the hardest and longest wins!

. . . .

HOW TO PLAY:

1. The players sit in a circle. One player is selected to start, and play proceeds clockwise around the circle.

2. Player One begins the game by saying "ha" in a very solemn manner. They neither smile nor indicate any merriment.

3. Player Two follows, saying "ha ha" with the same solemnity.

4. Player Three continues the pattern, saying "ha ha ha."

5. Players are out if they smile, laugh, or otherwise break from the serious nature of their endeavor. They are also out if they say "ha" the wrong number of times.

6. The player who lasts the longest wins.

VARIATIONS:

One variation has players alternating "ha," "ho," and "hee" instead of adding one more "ha" on their turn. The additional vowel sounds are a great opportunity to pull funny faces during your turn.

Another variation has all players solemnly proclaiming "ha" in unison. Nothing breaks the solemnity of a group chanting more than trying to suppress laughter.

WINK MURDER

Alternative Names: the Winking Game, Murder

Number of Players: 6+

Roles: the murderer, the victims

Supplies Needed: a deck of cards

. . . .

Everyone loves a good murder mystery! Players can live out their Sherlock Holmes daydreams by solving the mystery of who is murdering their fellow partygoers.

Wink Murder lives on in popular social games such as Mafia and Werewolf. The concept has taken on an even larger life with murder mystery dinner parties, where participants playact as different characters and often wear costumes. One (or more!) of their party dies during the dinner, and players must play detective to solve the mystery of the murdered guests.

Wink Murder is a highly adaptable game that can be played at parties, in classrooms, while camping, and more.

. . . .

HOW TO PLAY:

1. The players sit in a circle, possibly around a table.

2. From the deck, draw as many cards as there are players. The cards should all be number cards, with the exception of one jack.

3. Shuffle the cards and deal one to each player.

4. Whoever takes the jack is the murderer and must keep their identity secret.

5. The murderer attempts to wipe out the other players by winking at them.

6. If a player is winked at, they must make their death clear to the rest of the party. This includes extravagant moans and groans, convulsions, and so forth, growing more and more dramatic as the game progresses.

7. If a player believes they have caught the murderer in the act, they may accuse the murderer. If they're correct, the murderer must show their card. If incorrect, the accuser dies immediately.

8. The game is over when either the murderer
has successfully wiped out all the players or
the living players have correctly identified the
murderer.

VARIATIONS:

Another version of Wink Murder doesn't even involve playing cards! The detective and murderer are determined by drawing pieces of paper out of a hat (one piece says "detective," another says "murderer," and the rest are blank), and the game proceeds as above.

The detective is the one who tries to determine who the murderer is, rather than any player. The detective gets three guesses, and if all three are unsuccessful, or if the murderer winks at the detective, the murderer wins.

WINK POUT TWITCH

Wink Pout Twitch is a variation for a large group. The setup is the same, with roles drawn from a hat, but this time there are three murderers—one who kills by winking at their victims, another by pouting, and a third by twitching. The victims must be attacked by all three murderers before they die and are eliminated from the game.

Rather than dying extravagantly, they indicate how they have been killed in different ways. If attacked by the winker, the victim raises their right arm; if attacked by the pouter, they cross their legs; if attacked by the twitcher, they raise their left arm. Any player can call out who the murderer is, provided that they weren't the victim of the attack in question.

FORFEITS

Number of Players: 4+

Roles: the auctioneer, the players

. . . .

Forfeits are often thought of as a punishment for losing other games or committing another sort of misdemeanor—laughing during Throwing the Smile or the Laughing Game may result in handing over a favorite ring, or perhaps the unmasked murderer in Wink Murder forfeits their house key.

Here, however, forfeiting possessions becomes a game in its own right. Modern players should beware of forfeiting items of great value, unless they want to see their phone going home with a friend.

. . . .

HOW TO PLAY:

1. One player is selected to be the auctioneer and stands at the front of the room with a bowl.

2. The rest of the players place a personal item (keys, coin, wedding ring, etc.) into the bowl.

3. The auctioneer reaches into the bowl and pulls out an item. They present the item as though it were on sale and say this verse: "I have a thing and a very pretty thing. And who is the owner of this very pretty thing?"

4. The object's owner claims it.

5. The auctioneer then sets a price for the object's return. This can be as simple as singing a song or doing five jumping jacks.

6. After completing the challenge, the player retrieves their object. The aim of Forfeits is for all players to reclaim their objects.

POTENTIAL PRICES:

Take your group's makeup into consideration when selecting prices. If players are in any way uncomfortable with completing a task, offer an alternative. Obtain your fellow players' consent before assigning any tasks that involve touching another player.

- Sing a song.

- Tell a secret.

- Perform a dance.

- Yawn until someone else yawns.

- Do five jumping jacks.

- Run through multiplication tables.

- State whether you would prefer to eat an alligator or be eaten by one, and include your reasons.

HOT BOILED BEANS AND BACON

Alternative Names: Hot Buttered Beans, Hot Fava Beans, Hot Peas and Butter, Hide Objects, Hide Keys, Hot and Cold, Hide-and-Seek

Number of Players: 3+

Supplies Needed: a small object to hide, such as a card, a book, a ribbon, a thimble

. . . .

Likely thanks to its very silly name, Hot Boiled Beans and Bacon has had a remarkably long shelf life.

Hot Boiled Beans and Bacon makes an appearance in books like the 1865 adventure book *The Adventures of Reuben Davidger: Seventeen Years and Four Months Captive among the Dyaks of Borneo* by James Greenwood, wherein the titular character teaches his captors how to play the game. This, of course, utterly delights them.

It's also included in Charles Dickens's *The Mystery of Edwin Drood*. More modern audiences may recognize it from episodes of the 1990s sitcom *Full House*, the 2000s sitcom *The Big Bang Theory*, and the 2010s advice podcast *My Brother, My Brother and Me*.

. . . .

HOW TO PLAY:

1. One player leaves the space where the game is being played (or covers their eyes and counts to a large number, such as sixty or one hundred).

2. While they are distracted, the other players hide a small object. It can be hidden anywhere in the game space and does not need to be out in the open.

3. Once the object is hidden, the remaining players call the seeker back into the game space by chanting, "Hot boiled beans and bacon for supper; hurry up before it gets cold."

4. Once the seeker has returned, they begin their search. The rest of the players hint to the seeker the object's location by telling them "hot," "very hot," "scorching," and "burning" or "cold," "very cold," and "freezing," depending on how close they are to the object.

5. The game is over when the object is found.

VARIATIONS:

The game can also be played where one player hides the object and the rest seek. The player who finds the object is then the next to hide it.

There are a number of rhymes that can be used to call the seeker back in. These include:

- "Hot boiled beans and bacon, it's hidden and can be taken."

- "Little pigs come to supper, hot boiled beans and ready butter."

- "Hot beans and butter! Please come to supper!"

- "Hot boiled beans and very good butter! Ladies and gentlemen, come to supper."

- "Vesey vasey vum, Buck-a-boo has come! Find it if you can and take it home, vesey vasey vum."

The last of the list comes from Newlyn West, near Penzance in Cornwall, and originates from before 1886. In this version of the game, the seeker is blindfolded.

SMELLS

Number of Players: 5+

Roles: the host, the smellers

Supplies Needed: an assortment of small vessels such as cups, glasses, or jam jars containing substances that give off an odor; blindfolds; a pencil and paper

. . . .

Smells is a delightfully silly game. It's recommended to choose items with a strong but indistinct odor, such as strawberry jam over oranges, an apple slice instead of ammonia. This way, the smells are not as obvious, which makes for a sillier game.

Do be sure not to use harmful substances and chemicals. Additionally, please check with participants about allergies, sensitivities, etc. Nothing ruins a game night quite like a visit to the hospital.

. . . .

HOW TO PLAY:

1. The host prepares an assortment of vessels containing strong-smelling substances.

2. The smellers leave the room. They return one by one to be blindfolded and smell each vessel individually. The host records their guesses.

3. After making their guesses, the smellers remain in the room to watch the fun as the rest of the players smell the various substances.

4. The smeller with the most correct guesses wins.

SOME SUGGESTED SMELLS INCLUDE:

Strawberry jam	Chamomile tea
An apple slice	Basil
Honey	Lavender
Shoe polish	Lemonade
Custard powder	Pomade
Vinegar	

VARIATIONS:

While not a strictly Victorian version of the game, a variation on Smells can be played by tasting different foods or beverages while blindfolded. This version of the game has been memorably played on the comedy competition show *Taskmaster*.

Another variation is often played at modern-day baby showers. In this version, various substances are smeared inside baby diapers and players must smell each one to determine what they are.

CHARADES

Number of Players: 2+

Supplies Needed: a vessel to put clues in, pencils and paper

. . . .

Charades originated in sixteenth-century France and grew in popularity during the Victorian and Edwardian periods. The British embraced this game, and it became a fashionable after-dinner amusement.

Charades has a notable history in literature, having been used as a narrative device in Charlotte Brontë's *Jane Eyre* and William Makepeace Thackeray's *Vanity Fair.* J. M. Barrie, author of *Peter Pan*, and H. G. Wells, author of *The War of the Worlds*, were both enthusiastic players.

The game has maintained its popularity through the years due to its simplicity of play, its few props and minimal preparation, and its appeal for all ages.

. . . .

HOW TO PLAY:

1. On individual pieces of paper, players write two- or three-syllable words, then add them to a vessel.

2. On their turn, a player draws a slip of paper from the vessel and acts out the word on it for the audience to guess. The person who guesses correctly is the next to go.

For example, let's use the word *teacup*. The player might act out the second half of the word—*cup*—by cupping their hands together and miming taking a sip. For *tea* the player might mime brewing tea, pouring it into a cup, and sipping—with pinkie raised, of course.

VARIATIONS:

The Victorians were very fond of acting out nursery rhymes, poems, and proverbs. Players would act out a title or scene from a book or story, and often as a word game. This is how the game is played in Jane Austen's *Emma*. Emma asks Mr. Elton to contribute to Harriet's collection of conundrums, charades, and enigmas. Mr. Elton agrees and passes along the (at the time) famous charade:

My first doth affliction denote,

Which my second is destin'd to feel

And my whole is the best antidote

That affliction to soften and heal.

To solve this word puzzle, "my whole" is the word to be guessed, "my first" is its first syllable, and "my second" its second syllable. The answer: In the charade, "my first" is *woe* and "my second" is *man*, so "my whole" is *woe* + *man* = *woman*.

The modern version of Charades is a bit different from the traditional: Think of a book, television program, film, etc., and use hand signals to indicate what it is. Convey a book by opening hands like a book, for a film mime winding a camera, etc. Mime the title one word at a time. Signals can be added to help: Tugging on an ear means "sounds like"; tapping your fingers on your arm indicates that a word is broken up into syllables, and which syllable you are acting out.

ACTIVE GAMES

CHAPTER 2:

ACTIVE GAMES

If the energy of your gathering needs a little boost, these games are the solution! Active games are just that—active. These require large spaces to run around or move in. As they are delightfully silly and only slightly dangerous, it may be a good idea to have an ice pack or two on hand in case heads are bumped in Musical Statues or a player is a bit too enthusiastic in Are You There, Moriarty?

Many of the games in this section remain popular at children's birthday parties or as playground games, such as Musical Chairs or Pin the Tail on the Donkey. While some of these games are far older than the Victorian period, like Frog in the Middle, others may be a surprise to modern game players, such as the original rules for a Pillow Fight. These games are a fun challenge to get your heart rate up!

MUSICAL CHAIRS

Alternative Name: Going to Jerusalem

Number of Players: variable; the more, the merrier

Roles: the music director, the marchers

Supplies Needed: a device to play music (such as a CD player, phone, or piano), chairs (one fewer than the number of players)

. . . .

Musical chairs is a lively, scrambling game that is still played today. Initially, the music would have been provided by a pianist. The pianist could speed up or slow down the music at will, adding to the chaos!

The alternative name, Going to Jerusalem, comes from the German title of the game, Reise nach Jerusalem. The reason for this title is unclear, but it has been hypothesized that it could be a reference to the Crusades. The first known use of the name Musical Chairs to describe the game was in *Cassell's Family Magazine* in 1877.

. . . .

HOW TO PLAY:

1. Place chairs in a row. The chairs should alternatingly face in opposite directions.

2. The player in charge of the music begins playing it. The rest of the players march around the chairs in time with the music. They may not touch the chairs while marching.

3. When the music stops, the marchers scramble to find a seat. One player will not have a seat; they are "out."

4. A seat is removed so that once again there is one chair fewer than there are players. Play continues until the final chair is captured; the player able to secure the final chair is the winner.

VARIATIONS:

Chairs are placed in a circle, all chairs facing outward.

MUSICAL POTATOES

1. Players sit in a circle on the ground. Each player but one holds a potato in their right hand and behind their back.

2. When the music starts, each player passes their potato to the player to their left.

3. When the music stops, the player who is not holding a potato is eliminated.

4. A potato is removed so that once again there is one potato fewer than there are players.

5. Continue playing until the final potato is captured. The player holding the final potato is the winner.

SNAP-TONGS

1. Five players take part. Four chairs are set up in a circle, with four players seated. The fifth player (the "clock") holds a pair of tongs in hand.

2. The clock encourages the other players to dance around the chairs. While the other players are dancing, one of the chairs is removed from the circle.

3. The clock ends the dancing by "chiming" the hour by clicking the tongs together.

4. The other players scramble to sit in the chairs.

5. The player who is not seated once the time has been "chimed" becomes the clock, and the game continues until a player claims the final chair to win the game.

HARE AND HOUND

Alternative Names: Hunt the Fox, Three Deep

Number of Players: 6+, an even number

Roles: the hare, the hounds

. . . .

There are two different games called Hare and Hound. They are both active games where one player is chased by the other players. One can be played indoors. It is also known as Three Deep, which is a less violent name option.

The other variation is considered a boys' game and would have been played primarily by boys in the countryside due to its rowdy nature. Of course, we are not tied to Victorian gender norms, and anyone can play the game. This rowdier version was known as Hunt the Fox in Wales. The game mimics the once-popular tradition of fox hunting, which has fortunately grown significantly less popular due to its barbarous nature.

. . . .

HOW TO PLAY:

1. The players stand in a large circle in twos, one player behind another. Two players are left out of the circle; they are the hare and the hound. The hound aims to catch the hare.

2. The hare runs around the circle but at any point can stop and stand in front of a pair of players, making a line of three.

3. The player at the other end of this line becomes the hare, and the hound chases them instead.

4. The hound must continue chasing each successive hare until they catch one. The hound must not touch a hare who is standing in front of another.

5. If caught, the hare becomes the hound, and play continues until players are too tired to run anymore.

VARIATION:

Supplies Needed: a large space to run around in, paper

This variation is played in a large, outdoor space, maybe a playing field, park, lawn, or piece of picturesque countryside, using paper or something else that can be scattered during the game and easily cleaned up after.

One player is selected to be the hare, while the rest of the players are the hounds. The hare is given a head start of, say, fifteen minutes, and moves across the playing field, scattering paper to indicate their track.

Once the fifteen minutes are up, the hounds may begin to chase after the hare. The hare can employ any maneuver to try to shake the hounds off their trail, but they must continue to leave a trail so they can be followed.

The game is over when the hare either reaches home base (which should be decided upon at the start of the game) or is captured by a hound.

FROG IN THE MIDDLE

Alternative Names: Froggie in the Middle, Chytrinda

Number of Players: 5+

Roles: the frog, the taunters

Supplies Needed: a large open space to run around in

. . . .

The first reference to Frog in the Middle actually comes from a 1344 manuscript held by the Bodleian Library at Oxford University. The game is believed to come from an ancient Grecian game called Chytrinda, or "the cooking pot game." There is an illustration from a medieval manuscript that depicts four girls playing the game. Additionally, Frog in the Middle is the name of a Scottish country dance (or ceilidh) for eight or more dancers. But that's for a different book!

There are a number of games similar to Frog in the Middle, including the delightfully named Bull in the Park, "Fox in the Fold / Tod i' the Faul," and Bull in the Barn. The game is also very similar to Red Rover.

. . . .

HOW TO PLAY:

1. One player sits on the ground with their legs beneath them; they are the frog. The other players form a ring around them.

2. The rest of the players run around the frog, saying, "Frog in the Middle, you can't catch me."

3. The frog suddenly jumps out of the middle and tries to capture one of the other players. If caught, the other player becomes the frog. If not, the frog continues to try to catch another player.

4. The frog can only capture the other player by springing and grasping; they may not pursue their quarry.

VARIATIONS:

In one variation, one player sits on the ground with their legs crossed; they are the frog. The other players form a ring around them. The players in the ring around the frog try to push, pull, or buffet the frog while the frog tries to catch one of the other players without getting up. If caught, the other player becomes the frog.

In another variation, the selected frog stands at the center of a ring formed by the other players, whose hands are clasped. The frog tries to break through the ring using force while the other players endeavor to keep them in the middle. The players can do whatever they like but must keep their hands clasped. Once the frog escapes, they win the game!

There are a couple variations on the rhyme, including the following:

- "Frog in the Middle, you can't catch me."

- "Hey, hey, hi! Frog in the middle and there shall lie; he can't get out and he shan't get out—hey, hey, hi!"

- "Frog in the sea, can't catch me!"

THE SCULPTOR

Number of Players: 3+

Roles: the sculptor, the statues

. . . .

Sculpture was a major art form in the Victorian era, but it wasn't just marble busts on display in museums. Public sculpture flourished and sculptural portraits of many famous Victorians can still be seen in public spaces around London. It was only natural that game players would adapt themselves to this popular form of artistic expression, as we see in this game as well as Moving Statues and Musical Statues.

. . . .

HOW TO PLAY:

1. One player is selected to be the sculptor; the rest are the statues.

2. The statues all stand up around the room. The sculptor goes to each statue and puts them into an absurd and very silly posture. The posture must be maintained.

3. After completing their masterpieces, the sculptor goes to each statue and tries to make them laugh or move. The sculptor may do anything (with consent) short of touching anyone.

4. The first player to move or laugh becomes the new sculptor, and the game begins again.

5. Play continues until all participants have had a chance at being the sculptor.

MOVING STATUES

Alternative Names: Grandmother's Footsteps, Fairy Footsteps, Statues

Number of Players: 5+

Roles: the caller, the statues

Supplies Needed: an open space to play in, such as a field or gymnasium

. . . .

Moving Statues has made its mark on pop culture. The game inspired one of the most terrifying monsters in the current iteration of the British television series *Doctor Who*—the Weeping Angels. The Angels are monsters that can only move when not observed, casting the show's characters into the role of caller. It makes for very, very tense viewing, but your game doesn't have to be that scary!

. . . .

HOW TO PLAY:

1. One player stands at the head of the room with their back turned. They are the caller.

2. The other players advance toward the front of the room.

3. The caller may turn around at any point. When they do, the rest of the players must freeze in whatever position they are in. If any of the players move, even slightly, they must move to the back of the starting line and begin again.

4. The first person who gets near enough to touch the caller is the winner, and then takes over that role if the game continues.

VARIATIONS:

Moving Statues is a highly adaptable game. Players can make the game more or less cutthroat as desired. For example, one variation that makes the base game more difficult is if a player moves at all, they are immediately out. In another variation, the caller may walk among the statues and try to make them move by waving in their faces, trying to make them laugh, etc. However, with this rule in play, the statues themselves may move—so long as the caller's back is turned.

The game can also be played as Red Light, Green Light. The game play is identical, except the caller exclaims "Red light!" when the advancing players must stop and "Green light!" when they may move.

MUSICAL STATUES

Alternative Names: Statues, Freeze Dance

Number of Players: 11+, an odd number

Roles: the dancers, the musician

Supplies Needed: a device to play music
(such as a CD player, phone, or piano)

. . . .

Genteel Regency society wasn't ready for the waltz, with its risqué close embrace, but by the early Victorian era, the waltz had made inroads into ballrooms all over England.

Polka became an overnight sensation in 1844 after its 1843 introduction to Paris. The wholesome exuberance of the Bohemian dance made close partner dancing acceptable. This joyful dancing defined the early part of the era. Gradually, the polka and the various dances it inspired faded from popularity. By the 1870s, middle-class public balls largely featured only the waltz and the two-step; high-society balls were more interested in parlour games.

. . . .

HOW TO PLAY:

1. All players except one couple up to dance together. The uncoupled player is in charge of the music.

2. The music begins, and the couples dance with reckless abandon.

3. When the music suddenly stops, the players must remain stock still in whatever position they have found themselves. The music may start up again at any point.

4. Any player who moves—even so much as a smile—disqualifies their couple.

5. The couple who is able to stay still the longest wins.

VARIATIONS:

This game can easily be played with players competing as individuals rather than couples. This version may make it easier to avoid catching another player's eye and dissolving into laughter.

Thanks to the wonders of modern technology, the game can also be played with as few as two people. YouTube is full of videos with kid-friendly music that starts and stops at random intervals for this very purpose.

FEEDING THE BABY

Number of Players: 2

Supplies Needed: two blindfolds; two bowls of broken biscuits, crumbled cake, or cornflakes; two wooden spoons; a vacuum for cleanup

. . . .

If you're looking for a silly game to play, look no further than Feeding the Baby. It works well with large numbers, as only two people play but the rest of the group can join in the merriment by watching and laughing along.

The irony is that child-rearing in the Victorian era was often authoritarian and grim. However, it is also during the Victorian era that the modern concept of childhood was established. Society recognized that children and adults were separated by different wants and needs. Child labor laws came into effect, and school became required. A market for children's literature and fairy tales emerged. Victorian authors like Charles Dickens wrote books where children were likable, vulnerable, and needed to be cared for by loving adults.

. . . .

HOW TO PLAY:

1. Two players are blindfolded and sit on the floor with their knees touching. Each is given a bowl filled with crumbled food and a spoon.

2. On "go," the two players attempt to feed each other. They try to fill their spoons and then steer them into the other's mouth. Naturally, more of the food will end up on the floor, or the players' laps, than in their mouths.

3. The game ends when one of the players has run out of food to serve their partner, or when everyone is laughing too hard to complete the task.

As with all games involving food, please check with participants for dietary restrictions. Soft foods work best, and be sure to use a plastic or wooden spoon so no one gets hurt.

SOME SUGGESTED FOODS TO USE:

- Cooked rice
- Oatmeal
- Ice cream
- Yogurt
- Cereal in milk
- Mashed potatoes
- Any other food that's easy to spoon and fun to eat!

This is a very messy game, so do have your cleaning supplies ready to go.

PILLOW FIGHT

Number of Players: 3+

Roles: 2 blindfolded players, 1 or more secret players

Supplies Needed: two blindfolds, one pillow for each player

. . . .

Ah, the pillow fight! A staple of sleepovers, both real and fictional. Who can forget the images of feathers flying through the air as players are hit by pillows?

One of Thomas Edison's 1897 experiments in filmmaking featured a pillow fight. Four girls, each equipped with a pillow, take turns hitting each other while jumping around on beds on a soundstage. They begin by taking turns, but by the end of the short film, they are hitting each other willy-nilly.

Additionally, modern readers may be pleased to hear that pillow fighting is now a competitive contact sport. It is played professionally, often in a wrestling ring. Of course, none of the players are blindfolded in a professional competition.

. . . .

HOW TO PLAY:

1. This game works best in a group large enough for the two blindfolded players to not know how many secret players are in the mix.

2. Two players are blindfolded. They are put in opposite corners of the room and each given a pillow. The players are informed that they will receive a point for every time they hit their opponent.

3. They advance toward each other.

4. Unbeknownst to either of them, one or more secret players have been given a pillow, and they are not blindfolded. The secret players hit the two blindfolded players to confuse them, and they hit back on presumably empty air.

5. The game ends when the players are too tired to continue.

VARIATION:

Another way to have a pillow fight is to have a free-for-all. All members of the party are equipped with a pillow, no one is blindfolded, and everyone may hit each other with the pillows.

Participants may choose to enact safety rules—no hitting above the chest, no sweeping the legs, etc.— and limit just how much time is spent having the pillow fight.

ARE YOU THERE, MORIARTY?

Number of Players: 3

Roles: the players, the referee

Supplies Needed: two blindfolds, two rolled-up newspapers or magazines or other soft bludgeoning instrument (a pillow, perhaps)

. . . .

The origin of Are You There, Moriarty? is hotly debated. One theory suggests that the game was named for the Napoleon of crime, Professor Moriarty, from Sir Arthur Conan Doyle's Sherlock Holmes stories. In the stories, Moriarty is Holmes's archnemesis, and the two wrestle to their presumed deaths at Reichenbach Falls in the 1893 short story "The Final Problem."

Another theory suggests that the game was named for the 1876 musical hall song "Are You There, Moriarty?," which follows an affable Irish cop who is more interested in charming the ladies than doing his job.

The game was played in David Nicholls's book *One Day* and its movie adaptation.

. . . .

HOW TO PLAY:

1. Two players are blindfolded and each equipped with a rolled-up newspaper. They lie down on their stomachs an arm's length apart and grasp each other's left hand in an arm wrestling position. In their right hands, they hold the rolled-up newspapers.

2. The game begins when Player One asks, "Are you there, Moriarty?" Player Two responds, "I am here." Player One then brings their newspaper down where they believe Player Two's head is. The referee determines whether it is a hit or a miss. If Player One successfully wallops Player Two, they are permitted another go. If they miss, it is then Player Two's turn. Player Two then asks, "Are you there, Moriarty?"

3. Players are encouraged to deceive their opponents. They can move their heads after responding, whisper, anticipate opponents' moves, and so forth. Players may roll around but not get up. Their hands must remain locked at all times.

4. The referee may choose to retire a player early if they determine it to be necessary. A winner is declared when a player gets a clean wallop on their opponent's head. If more than two are playing, a new contestant opposes the winner.

VARIATION:

The game can also be played seated in chairs, as it was memorably played on the BBC panel show *QI* during the 2016 Christmas episode, which might make a more accessible way to play.

PIN THE TAIL ON THE DONKEY

Alternative Names: Putting the Tail on the Donkey, Tailless Donkey, Donkey Party

Number of Players: 3+

Supplies Needed: a picture of a donkey without a tail, cutouts of a donkey's tail equivalent to the number of players, a blindfold, pins or tape

· · · · · ·

Pin the Tail on the Donkey was invented in Milwaukee in the mid-1880s. By 1887, it was a craze that had spread throughout the United States. Anyone who was anyone, from women's clubs to society dinners to charity events, hosted a donkey party. Enterprising entrepreneurs such as Charles Zimmerling capitalized on the game's popularity, creating kits for ease of playing. The game captured a nation and is still played to this day.

· · · · · ·

HOW TO PLAY:

1. The host hangs a picture of a donkey who is missing its tail. This can be either purchased or drawn by the host.

2. Each player takes a false tail, with a pin or piece of tape to affix it to the donkey. The player whose turn it is to pin the tail on the donkey stands six feet away from the donkey. The player is blindfolded, possibly spun around, and sent walking toward the donkey. The player endeavors to attach the tail to the donkey's rear end.

3. Each player takes a turn to try to pin the tail on the donkey. After all tails have been placed, the players see who pinned the tail closest to the correct location. The player with the tail closest to the donkey's behind receives a prize like a small present, and the player whose tail is farthest away or in the silliest location wins a "booby prize," which may be a punishment or just getting laughed at.

VARIATIONS:

It's very easy to update Pin the Tail on the Donkey to your party's theme. A Halloween party might play "Put the face on the jack-o'-lantern" or a baby shower may have "Put the diaper on the baby," and so on.

For added difficulty, try using an image with more than one item that needs to be pinned in one of several specific spots. Play "Pin the feature on Frankenstein's Creature" and see where the eyes, nose, and mouth end up.

TABLE GAMES

CHAPTER 3:

TABLE GAMES

After an afternoon of running around playing Musical Chairs, or a healthy bout of a Pillow Fight, quieter games may be desired. The games in this section can all be played while sitting at a table, perhaps while having tea or drinks with friends. The table games included require a bit of concentration (even and especially the game Concentration!), so being more than a couple drinks in may prove detrimental.

The games in this section largely require some preparation, primarily providing decks of cards, timers, and/or sheets of paper and pencils as needed.

CELEBRITIES

Number of Players: 4+

Roles: the leader, the listers

Supplies Needed: a timer, pencils and paper

· · · · · · · · · · · · · · · · ·

The Victorian era saw the dawn of a new age of celebrity culture, one that transcended even reality.

Sherlock Holmes feels synonymous with Victorian London in a way that few *real* people do. Sir Arthur Conan Doyle spent six years writing the many adventures of Holmes and Watson, but in 1893 Doyle decided to kill off the famous detective in his short story "The Final Problem." He could hardly have predicted the response.

Holmes's fans would have none of it. Many openly mourned the detective's demise by wearing black mourning bands, twenty thousand readers canceled their subscriptions to *The Strand Magazine*, where Sherlock Holmes stories were regularly published, and even the royal family was shocked. After ten years of public demand, Conan Doyle revived Holmes in the story "The Adventure of the Empty House." He would continue to write the consulting detective's stories until 1927.

· · · · · · · · · · · · · · · · ·

HOW TO PLAY:

1. A leader is chosen; the other players receive pencils and paper.

2. The leader selects a letter of the alphabet—for example, *G*. The players then have three minutes to write down as many celebrities as they can whose names begin with *G*. Celebrities may be actors, musicians, writers, politicians, criminals, public figures, etc. The leader will be the last voice on any disputes about whether or not someone is a celebrity.

3. After the three minutes are up, everyone reads their list of celebrities. Each celebrity who does not appear on any other list is granted one point. For example, if one player says "Gandhi," then all other players must cross Gandhi off their lists.

4. The player with the highest score wins. One strategy is to come up with lesser-known celebrities. Gandhi, Gigi Hadid, and Lady Gaga may be eliminated much quicker than H. R. Giger, Artemisia Gentileschi, or Zsa Zsa Gabor.

VARIATIONS:

Celebrities is an easy game to adapt for different situations. Much like Pin the Tail on the Donkey, the theme can be changed for the party. A children's party may have "Disney characters whose names start with *G*" (Gaston, Goofy, Grumpy), or a cinephile party could be "Oscar winners that start with *G*" (*The Godfather*, *Get Out*, Alec Guinness).

DOUBLETS

Alternative Name: Word-Links

Number of Players: 1+

Supplies Needed: pencils and paper

. . . .

The game of Doublets was invented by author Lewis Carroll (the nom de plume for mathematician, author, and logician Charles Lutwidge Dodgson). Carroll devised Doublets in 1877 as a game for two of the children he was friends with, at the time calling it Word-Links. After testing the game with family and friends, he devised a set of rules. The puzzle appeared in the March 29, 1879, edition of *Vanity Fair*, a British weekly society magazine known for its witty prose and social commentary on British life.

Carroll regularly provided samples of doublets in subsequent issues until 1881, along with his own solutions and occasional comments on the rules.

He delighted in games and wordplay. Along with the two Alice books (*Alice's Adventures in Wonderland* and *Through the Looking-Glass*), Carroll wrote mathematical treatises, nonsense poetry, and other novels for children.

. . . .

HOW TO PLAY:

1. The rules of Doublets are simple, but the game itself is not.

2. Two words with the same number of letters are proposed. The challenge is in linking the words together with words of the same length that vary by only one letter.

3. The letters cannot be rearranged within the word.

4. The puzzle is complete when the starting word has been turned into the finishing word.

5. The player who completes the transposition with the fewest number of link words wins the round.

EXAMPLES:

Below are examples of Carroll's own puzzles and solutions.

PROVE A ROGUE A BEAST

ROGUE	Valve	Leave
Vogue	Halve	Lease
Vague	Helve	Least
Value	Heave	BEAST

EVOLVE MAN FROM APE

APE	Err	MAN
Are	Ear	
Ere	Mar	

STEAL COINS

STEAL	Sheer	Shins
Steel	Shier	Chins
Steer	Shies	COINS

GALLOWS

Alternative Names: Hangman, Hanging the Man

Number of Players: 2+

Roles: the hangman, the condemned

Supplies Needed: a pencil and paper

. . . .

Games like Gallows feel so perfectly morbidly Victorian. Death very much was a part of life for the Victorians, and they were obsessed with it, to the point that the mourning industry was massive. You could buy mourning teapots, mourning attire for all ages, and mourning stationery. Victorians would wear even jewelry made from a deceased loved one's hair.

Like with many games, the origin of Gallows is unknown. There is an apocryphal story that the game came into being as a way for the condemned to save their lives during the seventeenth century; however, the game likely comes from traditional British word games such as Birds, Beasts, and Fishes, where one player writes down the first and last letters of a bird, animal, or fish and uses *X*s to indicate the missing letters and length of the word.

. . . .

HOW TO PLAY:

1. The hangman chooses a word. For our example, the word is *charming* (eight letters).

2. They announce how many letters it has and proceed to mark on a sheet of paper the same number of letters as blanks. The letters are represented as such: _ _ _ _ _ _ _ _

3. The condemned asks the hangman if the word contains one letter; we will use *A* as an example.

4. Where the answer is yes, the hangman places the letter in the appropriate blank. In our example, it would look like this: _ _ A _ _ _ _ _

5. On their next turn, the condemned asks if the word contains another letter; for our example, say an *E*.

6. Where the answer in this case is no, the hangman begins to build the gallows.

7. The game continues until the condemned wins by discovering the word before the gallows is constructed and the hanging man completed, or until the execution is carried out.

CONSTRUCTION:

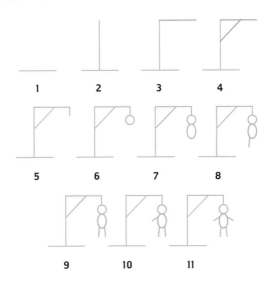

VARIATION:

PROVERBS GALLOWS

This variation of Gallows is played the same, except a well-known phrase is used instead of a single word. Using the phrase "A piece of cake," the letter spaces are laid out as such:

_ _ _ _ _ _ _ _ _ _ _ _

GUGGENHEIM

Alternative Name: Categories

Number of Players: 4+

Supplies Needed: pencils and paper

. . . .

Guggenheim is an enduringly popular parlour game of categories and alphabetical items. In fact, the more commonly played version in today's parlours is called Categories, but the Victorians played a slightly more sophisticated version of the game requiring pen and paper. The game is very easy to set up and play on the fly. Guggenheim has inspired many commercially available board games, such as Scattergories (which adds dice), Facts in Five, and Nomen.

. . . .

HOW TO PLAY:

1. The host selects a word of at least five to six letters in length, with no repeating letters. If, for example, the word is *France*, it is written down as in the diagram on page 106. (The diagrams can be made and printed for players ahead of time.)

2. As in the example, a number of various categories should be listed in the diagram. These are up to the discretion of the host.

3. All players must fill up their squares. First, they think of a town beginning with *F* (Fairfield, Frankfurt, etc.) before moving on to the letter *R*, and so on, and then the remaining categories.

Scoring is based on a predetermined rubric. There are a number of ways that the game can be scored:

- The person who completes their diagram first wins.

- The person who fills in the most squares in an allotted time period wins.

- The winner is the player who acquires the most points using the following system: one point for all the players who write the same answer (for example, everyone who puts down Frost as the poet), and ten points for any player who writes a unique answer. In this case, players will likely strive for odder choices.

VARIATIONS:

The categories and word choice are very easily customized. For example, the game could be played at a child's birthday party. The word could be the child's name (for example, THOMAS), and the categories would be based on their interests (books, musicians, sports teams, Pokémon).

A more risqué version could be played at a bachelorette party, with the bride-to-be's name as the word and the categories ranging from the sweet (honeymoon locations, flowers) to the saucy (types of lingerie, sex toys, and more).

EXAMPLE:

	F	R
TOWN	Fairbanks	Rome
BOOK	*Fahrenheit 451*	*Rebecca*
RIVER	Falémé	Rubicon
POET	Frost	Rilke
FLOWER	Foxglove	Ranunculus
SHAKESPEARE CHARACTER	Feste	Romeo

A	N	C	E
Athens	Nice	Copenhagen	Edinburgh
Animal Farm	*The Name of the Rose*	*The Call of the Wild*	*Emma*
Arno	Nile	Cagayan	Euphrates
Angelou	Nabokov	Carroll	Eliot
Aster	Nasturtium	Carnation	Echinacea
Antonio	Nerissa	Caliban	Emilia

SNAP

Alternative Name: Slap

Number of Players: 2–6

Supplies Needed: one or two packs of playing cards (one pack for 1–3 players, two packs for 4–6)

. . . .

Snap was commercialized in the 1880s by games company John Jaques and Son. The original deck by the company featured sixty-four cards, with illustrations by *Alice's Adventures in Wonderland* artist John Tenniel. The traditional Snap deck features four sets of fourteen different characters. The game was adapted for play with a regular deck shortly after.

John Jaques and Son was responsible for introducing a number of other games into the broader world. Jaques and Son produced the first official rules of croquet in the 1850s, as well as complete sets for playing. The company also released Ping-Pong sets after lawn tennis overtook croquet in popularity.

. . . .

HOW TO PLAY:

1. The cards are shuffled and dealt face down among the players. Players take the hands they have been dealt but may not look at them.

2. Moving clockwise from the dealer, each player in turn flips the top card from their hand and lays it flat in front of them. This continues until two of the exposed cards are the same face value— two kings, two twos, etc. Once this occurs, the owners of the two cards have the opportunity to yell "Snap!" The first of the two to do this takes all the cards played by both up to this point.

3. Players may only call "Snap!" when their own card coincides with another.

4. The game ends when one player holds all the cards. Should a player be left with one card, it remains on the table until it coincides with another. The holder must yell "Snap!" first when this occurs, or they lose their card and are out of the game.

VARIATIONS:

SLAPJACK

For those who crave violence with their card games, another version of the game follows identical rules with one exception: Instead of calling "Snap!" players say "Slap!" and slap the deck. There is the risk of getting your wrist slapped and coming away from the game bruised.

ANIMAL GRAB (3–6 PLAYERS)

The rules of this variation are nearly identical, with one difference. Each of the players is given a distinctive animal (cow, dog, cat, etc.), and instead of yelling "Snap!" the players must make the cry belonging to the other player's animal. The first player to give the correct cry wins the cards.

GRIMACE SNAP (3–6 PLAYERS)

In this variation, instead of yelling "Snap!" the two players facing off endeavor to make each other laugh. The players may not speak or touch the other player. The first to laugh loses their cards.

GRAB CORK OR SILENT SNAP (3-6 PLAYERS)

In this variation, instead of yelling "Snap!" the two players facing off aim to grab a cork in the middle of the table. Silent Snap is a good option for playing when relative quiet is needed, such as when others are napping or reading.

GERMAN WHIST

Alternative Name: Hamburg Whist

Number of Players: 2

Supplies Needed: one deck of cards, a pencil and paper

• • • • • • • • • • • • • • •

Whist is the ultimate British card game. Born in early eighteenth-century London coffee-houses, Whist's first rule book was written and published in 1742 by Edmond Hoyle. The rules laid out in Hoyle's *A Short Treatise on the Game of Whist* remained official until a new rule book, *The Laws and Principles of Whist Stated and Explained and Its Practice Illustrated on an Original System by Means of Hands Played Completely Through*, was released in 1862 by Henry Jones (who wrote under the pseudonym Cavendish).

Whist was an incredibly popular game and is highly referenced in literature from and about the Victorian era (and before). It is included in three of Sir Arthur Conan Doyle's Sherlock Holmes stories, in Edgar Allan Poe's "The Murders in the Rue Morgue," *Around the World in Eighty Days* by Jules Verne, and in Jane Austen's *Pride and Prejudice*, *Mansfield Park*, *Emma*, and *Sense and Sensibility*.

• • • • • • • • • • • • • • •

HOW TO PLAY:

German Whist is considered one of the easiest variations of the traditional game Whist, which is why the instructions for it are included here rather than those for the full Whist game. It incorporates all the basic principles of Whist. The game's objective is to reach or exceed the win target first (10, 25, 50 are the standard points).

The cards rank as follows (aces high): ace, king, queen, jack/knave, ten, nine, eight, seven, six, five, four, three, two. The four suits are equal in value, but the suit of the face up card has precedence over the other suits (the trump suit). For example, if the diamonds were trump, the two of diamonds would outrank the ace of hearts.

TERMINOLOGY:

Trump: the suit chosen by the last-dealt card that beats all other suits regardless of rank

Trick: one card played by each player

Hand: the round

Rubber: three hands

There are two stages per hand. The objective of the first stage is to better the thirteen-card hand you were dealt by winning as many trump cards as possible. The objective of the second is to win as many tricks as possible.

Tricks are created by each player playing a card into the middle. The winner of the trick is the player with the highest-ranked trump-suited card, or if no trump suit was played, the highest-ranking card of the card's suit.

STAGE ONE PLAY:

1. Each player is dealt thirteen cards, one card at a time.

2. The remaining twenty-six cards are placed face down to form the stockpile.

3. The top card is turned face up. This card's suit determines the trump suit for the hand.

4. The non-dealer plays first. They must decide whether they wish to win the face up card, which will bring it into their deck. To win the face up card, they play a card with a higher number. Whoever has the highest number

card—or a card in the trump suit—wins the face up card. Whoever loses gets the next card in the deck, which is kept face down until it is in the player's hand. This is called a trick.

5. The two cards played in the trick are discarded.

6. The aim of this stage is to acquire as many high-value cards as possible, including as many cards in the trump suit as possible.

7. Once thirteen tricks have been played and there are no more cards in the stockpile, the players move on to the second stage.

8. Each player now has thirteen cards in their hand, many of which will be different from the cards they began with.

STAGE TWO PLAY:

1. Player One places a card face up. It can be of any suit or value. In this example, Player One plays a six of clubs. The trump suit is hearts.

2. Keeping in mind the trump suit established in the first play of the game (hearts), Player Two selects a card and places it face up, trying to beat Player One's card. This can be a card of a higher rank in any suit or a trump suit card. Player Two has a seven of clubs that they can play. They play it and win the trick.

3. This continues for a total of thirteen tricks. The player who wins the most tricks wins the hand.

4. A card in the trump suit will beat a card of a different suit. For example, if Player Two plays an ace of spades, Player One can play the two of hearts and still win the trick.

SCORING:

Whoever wins the most tricks in stage two adds that many points to their total. The first person to ten, twenty-five, or fifty points—as decided on ahead of time—wins. Alternatively, players can opt to play a rubber, which is three hands.

CONCEN-TRATION

Alternative Names: Fish, Pelmanism, Memory, Matching Pairs, Match Match

Number of Players: 1+

Supplies Needed: one deck of cards, or more if a large group is playing

. . . .

Memory games were very popular in the Victorian era. Concentration is an easy game to set up because it involves only a deck of cards. Other memory games, like Kim's Game, which involves memorizing the contents of a tray, take up rather more space and preparation than a deck of cards. These days, memory games are often given themes, such as a particular movie or franchise. For the Victorians, memory games could be truly random.

. . . .

HOW TO PLAY:

1. The cards are shuffled and laid out in equal rows face down on the table.

2. The first player turns up any two cards. If they make a pair (same rank and suit color: for example, a queen of hearts and queen of diamonds, or a three of spades and three of clubs), they claim the cards and place them face down in front of themself. The player is then able to take another turn, repeating until they do not make a pair.

3. If the cards do not make a pair, the player returns them face down.

4. Play proceeds clockwise, with the next player selecting two cards to see if they match or not. After a few rounds, the players begin to remember where various pairs are on the board.

5. The game ends when all cards have been paired. The player with the most pairs wins.

VARIATIONS:

To make the game easier, the suit color does not need to match; only the number is needed.

To make the game harder, players can add a deck so that each card has to find its exact match.

To make the game quicker, it can be played solo.

To add some variety, try using something other than a standard deck of playing cards. For an extra creative spin, draw your own set of matching image pairs on pieces of paper.

ROMANTIC GAMES

CHAPTER 4

ROMANTIC GAMES

Ah, romance. A gentleman caller arrives, a bouquet of roses on the mantle. The Victorians, though we often think of them as prudish, certainly did not skimp on romance games. Games such as Blind Man's Buff and Frincy-Francy provided Victorians with the opportunity to steal kisses from or make contact with potential love interests. Interestingly, none of the roles in the following games are gendered, which opened the possibility of contact with romantic interests of any gender.

Many of the games in this section have the primary objective of kissing or holding other players, but modern players may want to stick to variations with less romantic objectives. This chapter provides adaptations to several of the games that are more inclusive of different players' comfort levels. Do tweak the rules and variations to suit your party.

BLIND MAN'S BUFF

Alternative Names: Hoodman Blind, Hoodwinke Play, Blindfolded Buff

Number of Players: variable

Supplies Needed: a blindfold, enough space to move around without getting hurt

. . . .

Blind Man's Buff is a very old game, dating back as far as the Middle Ages, and variations of it are played around the world to this day. The game is first referenced by name in the late sixteenth century in the writing of actor and playwright Robert Wilson, though there are illustrations featuring the game dating back to the fourteenth century in Europe. Often misheard as "Blind Man's Bluff," the correct title is Blind Man's Buff. *Buff* is the Middle English word for "blow" or "buffet."

Social norms have changed since the Victorian era, not to mention the Middle Ages, and modern game players may want to opt for the less ableist and equally descriptive alternative name "Blindfolded Buff."

Blind Man's Buff makes many, many appearances in literature. Samuel Pepys writes about it in his diary in 1664, recounting the game being played at a Christmas party. The game is featured in *A Christmas Carol*, where it's played by Ebenezer Scrooge's nephew at his Christmas party. William Blake wrote a 1783 poem titled "Blind-man's Buff," which describes villagers playing a number of games, ending with Blind Man's Buff. The game is also the subject of many works of art, including numerous paintings by Jean-Honoré Fragonard.

In the eighteenth century, the game became a symbolic arena for courtship and chance. This symbolism directly relates to the idea that "love is blind." Although nothing about the game play is explicitly romantic, especially in some of the variations, it was a favorite among romantics. Because the object of the game is to touch, it was a fantastic opportunity for young lovers to grasp and hold each other in public.

. . . .

HOW TO PLAY:

At its heart, Blind Man's Buff is a game of tag with a twist.

1. To begin, one player volunteers to be blindfolded first or is chosen by lot. They are then turned around three times. After being properly disoriented, they are released to catch another player any way they can.

2. The other players tease the player mercilessly by pushing them, tickling their face with a feather, pulling their clothes, and so on.

3. Upon seizing someone, the blindfolded player guesses who it is they've captured. If they're correct, their prisoner becomes the next to don the blindfold. The game continues until participants decide they no longer want to play.

VARIATIONS:

FRENCH BLIND MAN'S BUFF

French Blind Man's Buff is nearly identical to Blind Man's Buff, except for two details. The blindfolded player additionally has their hands tied behind their back, and they must walk backward. They capture their prisoner by merely touching them.

THE BELLMAN

In this version, everyone is blindfolded except for one player. This player carries a small bell, which they ring occasionally. The blindfolded players all attempt to capture the bell ringer and more often than not succeed in capturing each other. When the bell ringer is successfully captured by a blindfolded player, that player becomes the new bell ringer.

This version of Blind Man's Buff came from a game played at a country fair. In its original incarnation, the role of the bell ringer was played by a belled pig.

ANIMALS

All players except the blindfolded player go to different parts of the room. The blindfolded player feels their way around the room until they touch someone. The person who has been touched must imitate an animal—dog, cat, rooster, donkey, etc.— repeating the sound up to three times if asked. The blindfolded player guesses the name of who it is they've found, and if they're correct, the person named takes the blindfold next.

I LOVE MY LOVE

Number of Players: 4+

. . . .

Etiquette dictated every element of life for the Victorians, and courtship was no exception. Both men and women followed strict rules to maintain and protect their reputations. There were appropriate hours for men to visit their intendeds; if the couple were meeting outside the home at a ball or concert, a chaperone was required. Couples did not get much time alone, and they did not get much opportunity to learn their beloved's private character.

This game is one of several played in Charles Dickens's *A Christmas Carol*, at the Christmas party thrown by Scrooge's family.

Scrooge's niece was not one of the blindman's buff party, but was made comfortable with a large chair and a footstool, in a snug corner, where the Ghost and Scrooge were close behind her. But she joined in the forfeits, and loved her love to admiration with all the letters of the alphabet.

. . . .

HOW TO PLAY:

1. The players sit in a circle and take turns posing questions about each other's imaginary loves. The group agrees on a set of questions in advance, such as "Why do you love your love? What will you give your love? Where did you meet your love? What did they feed you there? What is the name of your love? Where does your love live?" etc.

2. Players must answer with words beginning with the same letter.

3. The game begins with the letter *A* and continues through the alphabet.

EXAMPLE OF GAME PLAY:

Why do you love your love?
Because they are attentive.

What will you give your love?
I will give them an anorak.

Where did you meet your love?
In Austria.

What did they feed you there?
They fed me anchovies.

What is the name of your love?
Their name is Arthur.

Where does your love live?
They live in Aberdeen.

VARIATIONS:

There is a simpler version of I Love My Love where there is no back-and-forth question and answer. Instead, the players agree on a list of questions, and each person must answer all the questions at once, each player taking a different letter of the alphabet. The game plays as follows:

> A. I love my love with an *A*, because they are amiable, because their name is Andrew. I will give them an anchor, feed them on asparagus, and make them a bouquet of anemones.

> B. I love my love with a *B*, because they are brave, because their name is Betty. I will give them a book, feed them on butterscotch, and make them a bouquet of begonias.

And so forth, until the entire alphabet is played through.

Another variation of the game is even simpler. Played in a group, this variation continues with the alphabetical game, but the players pick adjectives without answering specific questions. The first player starts with the letter *A*, then the second player repeats the *A* and adds a *B*, and so on. For example:

Player One: I love my love because they are adorable.

Player Two: I love my love because they are adorable and bold.

Player Three: I love my love because they are adorable, bold, and caring.

Any of these variations can be played in groups of couples as a nice way for everyone to compliment their real-life partners. Modern players may also wish to play a less romantic version of the game, in which case it is perfectly all right to play "I love my friend," "I love my mother," or even "I love my cat."

THE PARROT

Alternative Name: To Perform the Parrot

Number of Players: 4+

Roles: the parrot, the teachers

. . . .

Birds were very popular pets for Victorians, and parrots were especially favored, their longevity amazing their owners. Victorian parrot owners would teach their birds to speak and say some very silly things. One famous talking parrot in Victorian literature is Captain Flint from *Treasure Island* by Robert Louis Stevenson. Captain Flint is Long John Silver's pet; the bird is fond of saying "Pieces of eight!" and is allegedly two hundred years old.

. . . .

HOW TO PLAY:

1. One player is assigned to be the parrot, either as a punishment for losing an earlier game or by drawing straws.

2. The parrot goes to each other player and says, "If I were a parrot, what would you teach me to say?"

3. Their fellow players can respond with whatever they would like, and the parrot must repeat.

4. Another player may also say, "Kiss, pretty Poll." When this happens, the parrot may kiss that player.

5. The game ends when the parrot has successfully kissed a player.

FRINCY-FRANCY

Number of Players: 4+

. . . .

Frincy-Francy was not often played in some of the highest-class parlours, as it was considered a game that lacked refinement. However, the game was very popular at parties held in country farmhouses. It was frequently played between dances.

As with all kissing games, please only play with those who have given their full consent. A player may change their mind. Additionally, the kisses do not have to be on the lips. They may be on the cheek, forehead, hand, and so forth, whatever players are most comfortable with.

. . . .

HOW TO PLAY:

1. Place a chair in the middle of the room. Player One sits in the chair.

2. Upon sitting down, Player One names another player whom they would like to kiss.

3. That player, Player Two, approaches the chair and kisses Player One, then takes the chair themself.

4. Player Two then announces whom they would like to kiss, and that player, Player Three, approaches them. The game continues until everyone has been well and truly kissed.

VARIATION:

Though not a direct variation, Spin the Bottle is a similar party game that originated in the 1950s. This more modern version of a kissing game takes the pressure out of announcing who you want to kiss.

HOW TO PLAY:

Players sit in a circle with a glass bottle in the center.

A player spins the bottle.

When the bottle stops spinning, the spinner kisses the person whom the bottle lands on.

After their kiss, the kissee becomes the spinner and the game continues.

THE BOX OF SECRETS

Alternative Name: *La Boîte d'Amourette* (The Box of Love)

Number of Players: 4+

Supplies Needed: a small box

. . . .

The Box of Secrets was a very popular game that originated in France under the name *La Boîte d'Amourette.*

The Box of Secrets is an excellent way to get forfeits from the players, which they then can compete for later in the evening. Of course, it also gives plenty of opportunities to kiss other players, which Victorians (and modern game players) appreciated.

As with all romantic games, please gain the consent of all players before commencing. Players may revoke consent at any time and/or opt for an alternative to being kissed on the lips.

. . . .

HOW TO PLAY:

1. The starting player, Player One, turns to their right-hand neighbor and presents them with the small box.

2. As they present the box, Player One says, "I will sell you my box of secrets; it contains three—whom I love, whom I will kiss, and whom I will send about their business."

3. The neighbor takes the box and replies, "I will buy your box of secrets. Whom do you love? Whom will you kiss? Whom will you send about their business?"

4. Player One then says the person in the party that they love, the person they intend to kiss (they may not be the same person), and the one they will send on their way.

5. The player to be kissed will be kissed on the spot.

6. The player who is sent about their business pays a small forfeit (an item to be won back at the end of the evening).

7. The buyer of the box then sells it to the player on their right, and the game continues until all players have sold and purchased the box.

VARIATIONS:

Kissing does not need to be on the lips. The player to be kissed may indicate where they would like to be kissed (cheek, hand, forehead, etc.). A kiss may also be blown to them.

Alternatively, one could use the opportunity to give the person to be kissed a small chocolate.

While not exactly an adaptation, this game bears a strong similarity to the modern classic Fu*k, Marry, Kill. A more refined group may want to stick to the Box of Secrets for a less vulgar version.

WORD GAMES

CHAPTER 5:

WORD GAMES

Whether you're stuck on a long journey, craving a guessing game, or wanting to entertain people of all ages, Victorian word games are just the ticket. The games in this chapter expand vocabularies, sharpen memory, and are very, very, very silly. Tell stories with your friends where the narrator changes at least once a minute, play with rhymes, delve deep into the treasures Grandmother's Trunk holds, and confound competitors with Yes and No.

Most of the games in this chapter require no preparation or materials, making them excellent options for playing whenever and wherever the fancy strikes.

YES AND NO

Alternative Name: Animal, Vegetable, or Mineral?

Number of Players: 2+

Roles: the selector, the guessers

. . . .

Many parlour games make appearances in Charles Dickens's *A Christmas Carol*. Scrooge is visited by the Ghost of Christmas Present, and together they invisibly join Scrooge's nephew's Christmas party. A variety of games are played, culminating in the party playing Yes and No. Scrooge himself is the subject of the game, and he is quite tickled by it!

The brisk fire of questioning to which he was exposed, elicited from him that he was thinking of an animal, a live animal, rather a disagreeable animal, a savage animal, an animal that growled and grunted sometimes, and talked sometimes, and lived in London, and walked about the streets, and wasn't made a show of, and wasn't led by anybody, and didn't live in a menagerie, and was never killed in a market, and was not a horse, or an ass, or a cow, or a bull, or a tiger, or a dog, or a pig, or a cat, or a bear.

. . . .

HOW TO PLAY:

1. The selector thinks of an object and keeps it to themself.

2. The guessers ask the selector questions about the object. The selector can only reply yes or no.

3. The game is over when the object has been successfully guessed.

EXAMPLE OF GAME PLAY:

Question: Are you an animal?

Answer: Yes.

Question: Do you have stripes?

Answer: No.

Question: Do you have spots?

Answer: Yes.

Question: Do you live on land?

Answer: No.

Question: Do you live in the sea?

Answer: Yes.

Question: Are you an orca?

Answer: Yes.

VARIATIONS:

The game may be played in reverse; one member of the party leaves the room, and the rest decide on an object for them to guess. When the player returns, they question the party. The party can only reply yes or no.

TWENTY QUESTIONS

Twenty Questions is the most famous variation of Yes and No. There is a limit on how many questions may be asked: twenty. If the guesser cannot hit upon the correct result within the allotted twenty questions, the selector continues in this role (with a new object) for the next round.

WHO AM I?

Number of Players: 4+

. . . .

Who Am I? is a very similar game to Yes and No. It has remained popular through the years and has inspired a number of different board and party games, including Hedbanz, Heads Up!, and more.

A version of this game was played with uncomfortable consequences in an episode of the American version of *The Office*. Parties wishing to enjoy this game should be sure to use terms and clues that will be fun for the whole party.

. . . .

HOW TO PLAY:

Each player secretly assumes the identity of a famous person. They are the celebrity.

In turn, each of the players asks the celebrity a question that is answered yes or no. This continues until it is discovered who the player is portraying.

EXAMPLE OF GAME PLAY:

Question: Are you a man?

Answer: No.

Question: Are you alive?

Answer: No.

Question: Are you a political figure?

Answer: Yes.

Question: Are you Queen Victoria?

Answer: Yes.

VARIATIONS:

One variation of the game has the celebrity leave the room. While they are out of the room, the rest of the players decide who they are. Upon returning, the celebrity needs to discover their identity by asking the questions.

In another variation, the players don't know who they are supposed to be. The celebrities' names are written on slips of paper (or tape, etc.), and each player holds one to their forehead so that they cannot read it, but the rest of the party can.

Each player takes a turn asking one question that is answered with a yes-or-no answer. Should they ask a question that is answered yes, they may ask another. If the question is answered no, their turn is over.

The game continues until everyone has discovered who they are.

HOW, WHY, WHEN, AND WHERE

Number of Players: 4+

. . . .

How, Why, When, and Where is yet another game played by Scrooge's niece in *A Christmas Carol* by Charles Dickens.

Likewise at the game of How, When, and Where, she was very great, and to the secret joy of Scrooge's nephew, beat her sisters hollow: though they were sharp girls too, as Topper could have told you. There might have been twenty people there, young and old, but they all played, and so did Scrooge; for wholly forgetting in the interest he had in what was going on, that his voice made no sound in their ears, he sometimes came out with his guess quite loud, and very often guessed quite right, too; for the sharpest needle, best Whitechapel, warranted not to cut in the eye, was not sharper than Scrooge; blunt as he took it in his head to be.

Grumpy Scrooge enjoys this game so much he begs the Spirit of Christmas Present to let him stay a bit longer, not wanting to miss out on the fun and games.

. . . .

HOW TO PLAY:

One player thinks of an object.

The other players try to discover what it is by asking these four questions—and asking each question only once:

- How do you like it?
- Why do you like it?
- When do you like it?
- Where do you like it?

VARIATION:

For a more difficult version, the first player may think of a word with homophones and use a different homophone in each reply in order to confuse their questioners. For example, they might use: *sight* (the power of seeing), *sight* (a thing one sees or that can be seen), *site* (an area), and *cite* (to quote by way of example):

- How do you like it? I like it clear.

- Why do you like it? I like it because it's regular.

- When do you like it? I like it on a sunny day.

- Where do you like it? I like it in a report.

CRAMBO

Alternative Names: Rhymes, Capping the Rhyme, ABC of Aristotle

Number of Players: 2+

. . . .

Crambo, a game where it helps to have a keen ear for rhymes, was one of the most popular of all Victorian parlour games. No party would be complete without playing a few rounds. It has been played in England since at least the fourteenth century, when it was known by the name ABC of Aristotle. The name Crambo itself made its earliest appearance in 1606, in writings by playwright and pamphleteer Thomas Dekker.

Eighteenth-century Scottish poet Robert Burns was an alleged Crambo fanatic. In his "Epistle to J. Lapraik," Burns uses the lines, "Amaist as soon as I could spell, / I to the crambo-jingle fell." James Boswell was another such enthusiast, and during the nineteenth century, Karl Marx was known to play the variation Dumb Crambo with his family. Samuel Pepys, the prolific seventeenth-century diarist, records on May 19, 1660, that people of all ages and situations played the game while traveling: "From thence to the Hague again playing at crambo in the waggon, Mr. Edward, Mr. Ibbott, W. Howe, Mr. Pinkney, and I." The game does not require any equipment, and that makes it a perfect game for the road.

. . . .

HOW TO PLAY:

1. The starting player, Player One, thinks of a word. They tell the guessers a word that rhymes with the chosen word.

2. The guessers ask questions about the chosen word.

3. Player One responds to each question with a sentence that ends in a word rhyming with the one they selected.

4. The game continues until either the guessers give the correct answer or Player One fails to give a proper rhyme.

5. Upon finishing the game, it can be continued with the guesser taking the role of the starting player.

EXAMPLE OF GAME PLAY:

In this example, the word selected is *thought*.

Player One: I know a word that rhymes with *jot*.

Guesser: Is it sweltering?

Player One: No, it is not hot.

Guesser: Is it a type of boat?

Player One: No, it is not a yacht.

And so forth.

VARIATIONS:

DUMB CRAMBO

1. The party splits into two teams. One team leaves the room and the other remains and decides on a word. This word must be a verb.

2. When Team One returns, they are told a word that rhymes with the word to be guessed. Team One must then act out the word they believe to be the answer. Should they get the answer incorrect, they are hissed at by Team Two.

3. They continue in this manner until the word is guessed and acted.

For example, the word selected is *look*.

Team Two tells Team One, "The word in question rhymes with *book*."

Team One believes the answer is *cook* and acts out a kitchen scene.

Team Two laughs at them, and Team One tries again.

CASSELL'S CRAMBO

Supplies Needed: pencils and paper

1. Each player writes a noun on one slip of paper and a question on another.

2. The slips are shuffled together, keeping the nouns and questions separate. Each player draws one slip at random from each category.

3. Players must answer the question by writing a verse that includes the noun.

EXAMPLE OF GAME PLAY:

Question: Why do summer roses fade?

Noun: Butterfly

"Summer roses fade away,

The reason why I cannot say,

Unless it be because they try

To cheat the pretty butterfly."

From *Cassell's Book of Sports and Pastimes*, 1882

GRAND-MOTHER'S TRUNK

Alternative Name: In My Grandmother's Trunk

Number of Players: 4+

. . . .

Grandmother's Trunk is a fun hybrid of a game. It's an alphabet game, like I Love My Love, and a memory game, like Concentration, combined with the comedy factor of the Laughing Game. It plays on the wonder and excitement of anticipating a grandparent's visit and wondering what presents they've brought. Not to mention, the game is good, silly fun. Just try not to laugh or you're out!

. . . .

HOW TO PLAY:

1. Players sit in a circle and take turns listing items kept in an imaginary grandmother's trunk. The items must each start with a different letter of the alphabet and, as such, do not need to be items normally stored in trunks.

2. The game continues in this manner through the alphabet. Each player must repeat the previous items in the trunk and add something silly to it at each turn.

3. Players are eliminated if they smile or laugh. They are also eliminated if they cannot recite what is included in the trunk.

EXAMPLE OF GAME PLAY:

"My grandmother keeps anchovies in her trunk."

"My grandmother keeps anchovies and a broom in her trunk."

"My grandmother keeps anchovies, a broom, and a castle in her trunk."

And so on.

VARIATIONS:

As with many parlour games, Grandmother's Trunk is one that is easily customizable based on age range. Themes can be applied to it, such as saying what is in a train car at a child's birthday or a diaper bag at a baby shower.

ELEPHANT'S FOOT UMBRELLA STAND

Number of Players: 4+

Roles: the leader, the purchasers

· · · · · · · · · · · · · · · · · · · ·

What exactly *is* an elephant's foot umbrella stand? During the Victorian era, big-game hunting rose in popularity, particularly with fashionable safaris in Africa. Like many Victorian pastimes, this came about as a result of British imperialism and colonization. The British colonial government in East Africa charged tourists fees to kill animals, and hunters came up with unique ways to display their trophies. One of these was to use a taxidermied elephant's foot to make an umbrella stand.

Today we know the harmful impact of nineteenth-century European hunters on African wildlife populations, but for the Victorians and Edwardians, the big-game hunters were colorful, romantic, and dashing figures. Allan Quatermain was one of the first Victorian literary adventure heroes, and his adventures began in H. Rider Haggard's *King Solomon's Mines* (1885). A less heroic example of a fictional big-game hunter appeared in Richard Connell's short story "The Most Dangerous Game," in which one American hunter finds himself the quarry of another who has grown tired of hunting animals in Africa.

If the idea of hunting takes the fun out of the game, not to worry. The starting item can be anything.

· · · · · · · · · · · · · · · · · · · ·

HOW TO PLAY:

1. The leader decides on a secret rule that each player must follow in order to have their purchases approved. In the example that follows, the rule is every object must end with the letter *D*.

2. The leader begins by saying, "I went to the store and bought an elephant's foot umbrella stand."

3. The player to the leader's left then says an object they think counts, such as, "I went to the store and bought a zebra chair."

4. When the player's purchase does not fit the rule, the leader says, "They are all out of zebra chairs."

5. Should the player decide to buy, say, a record, then the leader approves the purchase without saying why.

6. The purchases grow more and more silly as the game goes on. No one loses, but for fairness's sake the person who is last to catch on becomes the leader.

VARIATIONS:

The secret rule doesn't have to be based on the words themselves. A variation of the game could be physical, like the leader touching the side of their nose while saying the object. The rule could also be based around an upcoming event—for example, approved purchases could be doves, cakes, and rings if the leader has decided the rule is objects involved in planning a wedding.

ENDLESS STORY

Number of Players: 5+

Supplies Needed: a timer

. . . .

During the 1800s, magazine and pamphlet publishing boomed. Compulsory education in the United Kingdom led to a literate populace who craved light entertainment, and the burgeoning magazine market was there to provide. Sir Arthur Conan Doyle's famous Sherlock Holmes stories were regular features in the magazine *The Strand*. Novels like Charles Dickens's *Oliver Twist* and other longer works were also included in magazines, where they were often serialized to appear a chapter at a time. These serialized stories meant that readers had to wait for the next issue to find out what happens next, a tradition that continues on in television and comic books.

There is an entire genre of games that expand on Endless Story. The rules may be different or more complex, and the stories may not have endpoints at all. But the act of communally telling a story, of not knowing where it will go, is a very joyful thing. Tabletop role-playing games like Dungeons & Dragons, Vampire: The Masquerade, and Pathfinder carry on the spirit of Endless Story.

. . . .

HOW TO PLAY:

1. The players sit in a circle.

2. One player begins the story, any story at all, speaking for up to a minute. Without finishing the story, they touch the player to their right.

3. The player on their right then continues the story from whatever point it was left off at, even the middle of a sentence. Like their predecessor, they speak for up to a minute before passing to the person on their right.

4. This continues until the chain has reached the starting player again, who must conclude the story in less than a minute.

THE MINISTER'S CAT

Number of Players: 3+

. . . .

The Minister's Cat is another game that
has ties to *A Christmas Carol*. Though not
one of the many parlour games included in
the novel, the Minister's Cat is played in the
1970 musical film *Scrooge*, and its inclusion
launched a resurgence in popularity for the
game. The version played in the movie is the
Rhythm variation. This is an excellent game
for testing your memory, vocabulary, and
rhythm skills!

. . . .

HOW TO PLAY:

1. Players sit in a circle.

2. The first player describes the minister's cat with any adjective starting with the letter *A*. For example, "The minister's cat is an affable cat."

3. The player to their left goes next. They also describe the cat using a different adjective beginning with *A*. For example, "The minister's cat is an adorable cat."

4. This continues until the first player is reached again. At this point, the adjectives begin with *B*.

5. The adjective letter may also change once someone is eliminated from the game. Play continues in this way until all but one of the players are out.

6. Players are eliminated if they cannot find an adjective within five seconds or if they repeat one already used.

7. When you reach *X*, it is house rules as to whether or not you will permit words that begin with *ex*, such as *excellent*, or if they must begin with *x*, such as *xenomorphic*.

VARIATIONS:

In an easier version of the Minister's Cat, the adjective changes with each consecutive player (i.e., Player One is *A*, Player Two *B*, and so on). This would be a good version to play with small children who are just learning the alphabet.

RHYTHM:

The game can be made more difficult by adding clapping and knee slapping. Players must come up with an adjective before the final clap, otherwise they are out.

The rhythm is as follows, with italics representing a knee slap and bold, a clap:

The minister's **cat** is an *adjective* **cat**.

INCREASED DIFFICULTY:

The difficulty of the game can also increase by having the next adjective begin with the final letter of the previous adjective. For example:

Player One: "The minister's cat is a lovable cat."

Player Two: "The minister's cat is an erudite cat."

CHANGING DIRECTION:

Following the rules of the Increased Difficulty game, if an adjective begins and ends with the same letter, it can act as a reverse. In the above example, where Player Two says that the minister's cat is an erudite cat, the word ending in *e* means it returns to Player One instead of going to Player Three and the game moves counterclockwise instead of clockwise.

SOURCES

"14 Parlor Games to Bring Back This Holiday Season." *Mental Floss*, 15 Nov. 2016, https://www.mentalfloss.com/article/88659/14-parlor-games -bring-back-holiday-season-plus-one-you-definitely-shouldnt.

"Anyone Knows Any 'Social Game' Similar to Mafia or Werewolf? | BGG." *BoardGameGeek*, https://boardgamegeek.com/thread/632060/anyone -knows-any-social-game-similar-mafia-or-were. Accessed 1 Mar. 2024.

Augarde, Tony. *The Oxford A to Z of Word Games*. Oxford University Press, 1994.

Beaver, Patrick. *Victorian Parlor Games*. Magna Books, 1995.

CASSELL'S BOOK OF INDOOR AMUSEMENTS, CARD GAMES, AND FIRESIDE FUN. Third Edition, Cassell, Petter, Galpin & Co.:, 1881.

"Cassell's Family Magazine 1877." *Victorian Voices*, https://www.victorian voices.net/magazines/CFM/CFM1877.shtml. Accessed 1 Mar. 2024.

Child, Lydia Maria. *The Girl's Own Book*. W. Tegg & Company, 1856.

Coppercod - Play Free Card Games Online. https://coppercod.games. Accessed 1 Mar. 2024.

Crambo | Children's, Rhyming, Guessing | Britannica. https://www.britannica .com/topic/crambo. Accessed 1 Mar. 2024.

Definition of SPIN THE BOTTLE. https://www.merriam-webster.com /dictionary/spin+the+bottle. Accessed 1 Mar. 2024.

Dickens, Charles. *A Christmas Carol and Other Christmas Books*. Edited by Robert Douglas-Fairhurst, Oxford World's Classic paperback ed., Reiss, Oxford University Press, 2008.

Friedman, C. S. *Victorian Parlor Games and Activities*. Tridac Publishing, 2021.

"German Whist." *The Guardian*, 22 Nov. 2008. *The Guardian*, https://www .theguardian.com/lifeandstyle/2008/nov/22/rules-card-games-german-whist.

Gomme, Alice Bertha. *The Traditional Games of England, Scotland, and Ireland*. David Nutt, 1898.

---. *The Traditional Games of England, Scotland, and Ireland*. David Nutt, 1894.

History of Publishing - 19th Century, Mass Circulation | Britannica. https://www.britannica.com/topic/publishing/The-19th-century-and-the-start-of-mass-circulation. Accessed 1 Mar. 2024.

"Innocence and Ignorance: Concepts of Childhood Reflected in Charles Dickens' A Christmas Carol." *CLiC Fiction*, https://blog.bham.ac.uk/clic-dickens/2022/08/08/childhoodaca/. Accessed 1 Mar. 2024.

Ltd, Not Panicking. *H2g2 - "The Minister's Cat"- the Victorian Parlour Game*. 9 Nov. 2016, https://h2g2.com/entry/A87880783#conversations.

Melsom, Andrew. *Texts Are You There, Moriarty? : Debrett's House Party Games and Amusements*. Thames and Hudson, 1982.

"Murder Games ..." *The Guardian*, 23 Nov. 2008. *The Guardian*, https://www.theguardian.com/lifeandstyle/2008/nov/23/after-dinner-games-party-guide.

Nosowitz, Dan. "The Surprising Truth About Pirates and Parrots." *Atlas Obscura*, 19 Nov. 2015, http://www.atlasobscura.com/articles/the-surprising-truth-about-pirates-and-parrots.

Pendle, George. "Victorians' Christmas Parlor Games Will Leave You Burned, Bruised, And Puking." *Atlas Obscura*, 22 Dec. 2016, http://www.atlasobscura.com/articles/victorians-christmas-parlor-games-will-leave-you-burned-bruised-and-puking.

Periodicals - The Arthur Conan Doyle Encyclopedia. https://www.arthur-conandoyle.com/index.php/Periodicals. Accessed 1 Mar. 2024.

Rules of Card Games: German Whist. https://www.pagat.com/whist/german_whist.html. Accessed 1 Mar. 2024.

Sandison, George Henry. *How to Behave and How to Amuse. A Handy Manual of Etiquette and Parlor Games*. The Christian Herald, 1895.

"Saturday 19 May 1660." *The Diary of Samuel Pepys*, 19 May 2003, https://www.pepysdiary.com/diary/1660/05/19/.

Sherlock Holmes | Description, Stories, Books, & Facts | Britannica. 17 Feb. 2024, https://www.britannica.com/topic/Sherlock-Holmes.

"Snap Card Game - Traditional Snap Cards." *Jaques of London*, https://www.jaqueslondon.co.uk/products/snap-playing-cards. Accessed 1 Mar. 2024.

Squareman, Clarence. *My Book of Indoor Games*. Whitman Publishing, 1916.

Strutt, Joseph. *THE SPORTS AND PASTIMES OF THE PEOPLE OF ENGLAND*. 3rd ed., Thomas Tegg, 1845.

Temple, Emily. "A Few 19th-Century Parlor Games to Amuse You While You're Stuck at Home." *Literary Hub*, 30 Mar. 2020, https://lithub.com/a-few-19th-century-parlor-games-to-amuse-you-while-youre-stuck-at-home/.

The Book of Parlour Games: Comprising Explanations of the Most Approved Games for the Social Circle, Viz. Games of Motion, Attention, Memory, Mystification And Fun, Gallantry And Wit, With Forfeits, Penalities, Etc. H.C. Peck & Theo. Bliss.

The Victorians: Life and Death. https://www.gresham.ac.uk/watch-now/victorians-life-and-death. Accessed 1 Mar. 2024.

Thomas-Bailey, Carlene. "Charades - the All-Time Classic." *The Guardian*, 23 Nov. 2008. *The Guardian*, https://www.theguardian.com/lifeandstyle/2008/nov/23/7.

"Victorian Era Parlor Games." *Victorian Era*, https://victorian-era.org/victorian-era-parlor-games.html. Accessed 1 Mar. 2024.

"Victorian Pastimes & Recreations: Parlor Games & Indoor Amusements." *Victorian Voices*, https://www.victorianvoices.net/topics/recreation/games.shtml. Accessed 1 Mar. 2024.

ACKNOWLEDGMENTS

When I was younger, I thought of writing a book as a solitary endeavor. Now I realize just how mistaken I was.

Thank you to the wonderful team at Chronicle Books: my ever-patient and enthusiastic editor, Juliette Capra; eagle-eyed copyeditors Mary Paplham and Perry Crowe; designer Maggie Edelman; and the incredible artist Bene Rohlmann. Thank you all for making this book the most beautiful it could be.

Thank you to my family and friends, who kept me well caffeinated and reasonably socialized as I wrote. You listened politely as I recounted the rules to Are You There, Moriarty? yet again.

A final thank-you to Kieron Gillen and Jamie McKelvie, who I have yet to meet. Without their comic book series *The Wicked + the Divine*, this book would not exist.

ABOUT THE AUTHOR

Ned Wolfe is a queer author and artist whose subjects are heroes, health, and history. He lives in Cambridge, Massachusetts, surrounded by books, plants, and projects in various stages of completion. Ned swore an oath to protect the Bodleian Library, and he takes that very seriously.